Wise Words of STEAM

100 ENGINEERING WORDS EXPLAINED

JON RICHARDS

Cavendish Square

Published in 2025 by Cavendish Square Publishing, LLC
2544 Clinton Street, Buffalo, NY 14224

First published in Great Britain in 2021 by Wayland

Website: cavendishsq.com

Series editor: John Hort
Designed and edited by Tall Tree Ltd

Picture Credits
FC-front cover, BC-back cover, t-top, b-bottom, l-left, r-right, c-center
1–48 Sandra_M/Shutterstock.com, 4bl Maksim Shmeljov/Shutterstock.com, 5tr Daniliuc Victor/Shutterstock.com, 5br PTZ Pictures/Shutterstock.com, 5bl creator12/Shutterstock.com, 6tl Evannovostro/Shutterstock.com, 6bl Peter Sobolev/Shutterstock.com, 7c VectorMine/Shutterstock.com, 9tr Kozak Sergii/Shutterstock.com, 9cr Ljupco Smokovski/Shutterstock.com, 9b Dmytro Zinkevych/Shutterstock.com, 10–11 Voyagerix/Shutterstock.com, 11br David Antonio Lopez Moya/Shutterstock.com, 12bl Dervish45/Shutterstock.com, 12b JeepFoto/Shutterstock.com, 14tl CK Foto/Shutterstock.com, 14b Sion Hannuna/Shutterstock.com, 15tr Jason Finn/Shutterstock.com, 15cr Birdiegal/Shutterstock.com, 15bl Christine Bird/Shutterstock.com, 16c Pit Stock/Shutterstock.com, 17l Debbie Oetgen/Shutterstock.com, 17c wiangya/Shutterstock.com, 18c Gregory J Smith/Shutterstock.com, 18b Jodie Johnson/Shutterstock.com, 18br Pascale Gueret/Shutterstock.com, 19tl Ryan R Fox/Shutterstock.com, 19c Irina Mos/Shutterstock.com, 20c Sur/Shutterstock.com, 20–21b Luke Schmidt/Shutterstock.com, 21t INTREEGUE Photography/Shutterstock.com, 22t IZZ HAZEL/Shutterstock.com, 22b LO Kin-hei/Shutterstock.com, 23tr Frederico Rostagno/Shutterstock.com, 23tl Shutterstock.com/Love Lego, 23cr Alvov/Shutterstock.com, 23b Kuleshov Oleg/Shutterstock.com, 24tl Isaac Crabtree/Shutterstock.com, 24b mRGB/Shutterstock.com, 25c Nightman1965/Shutterstock.com, 25bl Songquan Deng/Shutterstock.com, 25br Mr. Amarin Jitnathum/Shutterstock.com, 26t Maksim Safaniuk/Shutterstock.com, 26b Gill Copeland/Shutterstock.com, 27t sakoat contributor/Shutterstock.com, 27b Stockr/Shutterstock.com, 28c EMFA16/Shutterstock.com, 29t Rudmer Zwerver/Shutterstock.com, 29br Foto-Ruhrgebiet/Shutterstock.com, 30t Rudy Balasko/Shutterstock.com, 30bl Gladysh Alexsandr/Shutterstock.com, 30br GREENWALDOS/Shutterstock.com, 31t aSuruwataRi/Shutterstock.com, 30–31c jamesteohart/Shutterstock.com, 32l SvedOliver/Shutterstock.com, 32r Markus Mainka/Shutterstock.com, 32b Sukpaiboonwat/Shutterstock.com, 33c Vera Larina/Shutterstock.com, 34c NChutchikov/Shutterstock.com, 35t Waldis Putnis/Shutterstock.com, 35bl Douglas Cliff/Shutterstock.com, 36c tele52/Shutterstock.com, 37tl Sergey Denisenko/Shutterstock.com, 37c topseller/Shutterstock.com, 37bl aragami12345s/Shutterstock.com, 38tl Vladi333/Shutterstock.com, 38br NASA/MSFC, 39t SpaceX/NASA, 39b Crew of STS-132/NASA, 40b zhengchengbao/Shutterstock.com, 41t Andrea Danti/Shutterstock.com, 41bl Everett Collection/Shutterstock.com, 41br hramovnick/Shutterstock.com, 42t Philip Lange/Shutterstock.com, 42b SkyLynx/Shutterstock.com, 43t SBWorldphotography/Shutterstock.com, 43c Evgeny_V/Shutterstock.com, 43b Francois BOIZOT/Shutterstock.com, 44t Sunshine Seeds/Shutterstock.com, 44b D.Uzunov/Shutterstock.com, 45tr PI/Shutterstock.com, 45l FreezeFrames/Shutterstock.com, 45b project1photography/Shutterstock.com, 46b Red ivory/Shutterstock.com, 47t Rabbitmindphoto/Shutterstock.com, 47c Syda Productions/Shutterstock.com, 47b Chaplin/Shutterstock.com.

Cataloging-in-Publication Data

Names: Richards, Jon.
Title: 100 engineering words explained / Jon Richards.
Description: Buffalo, New York : Cavendish Square Publishing, 2025. |
Series: Wise words of STEAM | Includes index.
Identifiers: ISBN 9781502671608 (pbk.) | ISBN 9781502671615 (library bound) |
ISBN 9781502671622 (ebook)
Subjects: LCSH: Engineering--Terminology--Juvenile literature.
Classification: LCC TA9.R53 2025 | DDC 620.003--dc23

CPSIA compliance information: Batch #CSCSQ25: For further information contact Cavendish Square Publishing LLC at 1-877-980-4450.

Printed in the United States of America

CONTENTS

DESIGNING AND DOING

The world around you is full of objects that have been designed and built using some sort of engineering, whether it's the cars and trains that take us from place to place, or the towering skyscrapers where people live and work.

1: *Engineering*

Designing and building machines, structures, and substances.

2: *Machine*

A device that is designed to help humans do something. Machines can be simple, such as a lever, or they can be made up of many parts, such as a car.

3: *Construction*

The building of an object, such as a car, a house, or a road.

FANTASTIC FACT

The ruins at Göbekli Tepe, Turkey, are the remains of one of the oldest buildings ever discovered. Studies show that it may have been engineered and constructed around 12,000 years ago!

SIMPLE MACHINES

The mechanical machines on these pages are designed to change the direction of a force, while making it easier to do a job.

4: *Wheel*

A circular object that spins around an axle and makes moving a load easier.

FANTASTIC FACT

The first wheels appeared nearly 5,500 years ago, but they were not used to transport things. Instead, they were potters' wheels and were used to make clay jars.

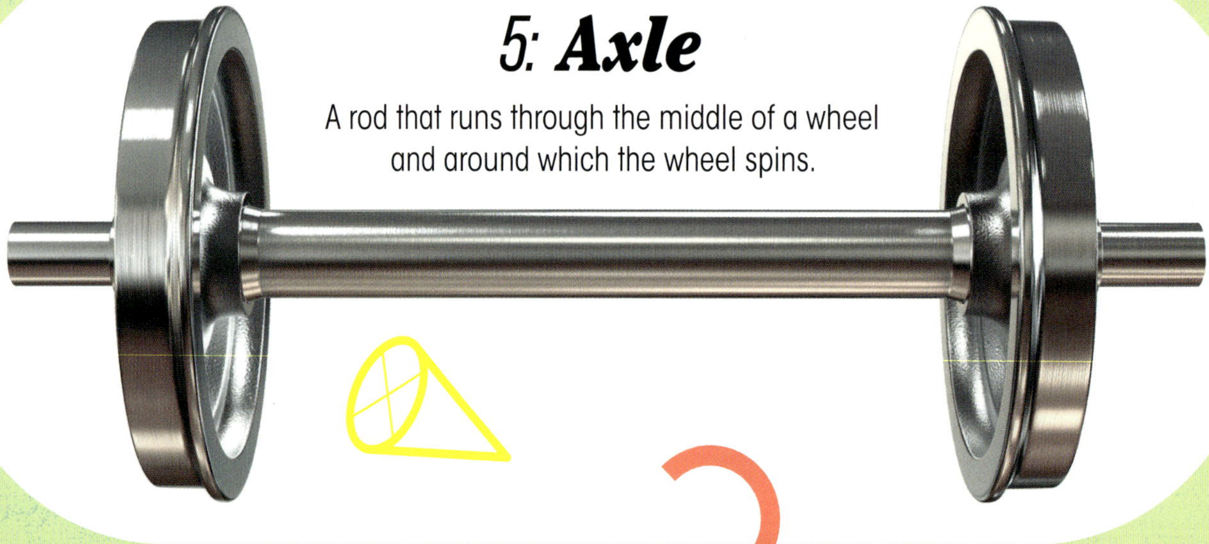

5: *Axle*

A rod that runs through the middle of a wheel and around which the wheel spins.

6: Pulley

A wheel around which a rope runs. The wheel changes the direction of a force applied to the rope, so a force pulling down on one end of the rope can result in a lifting force on the other end of the rope. Pulleys can be combined to increase the pulling force.

7: Effort

The force applied to a simple machine to move or lift an object.

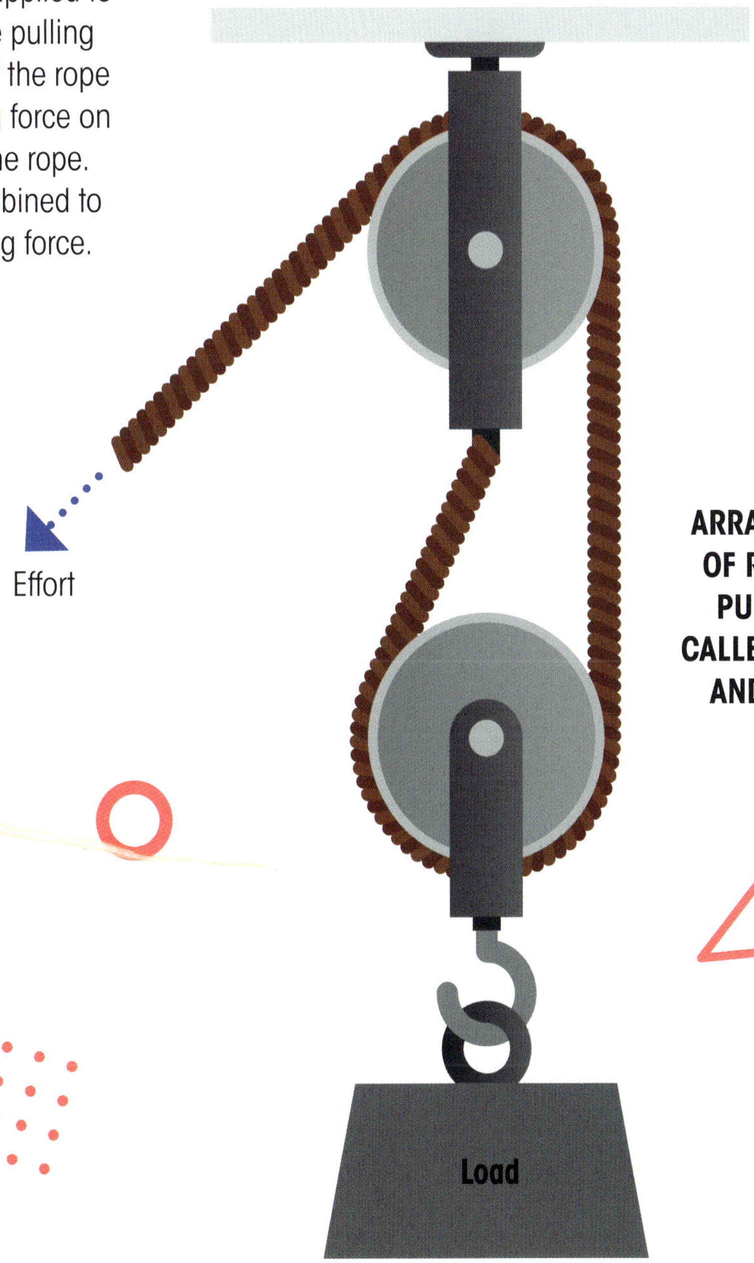

THIS ARRANGEMENT OF ROPE AND PULLEYS IS CALLED A BLOCK AND TACKLE.

8: Load

An item that is being moved or is about to be moved.

9: *Inclined plane*

A slope or ramp that makes it easier to move an object upward. The shallower the angle of the slope, the easier it is to move the object, but the further it has to travel.

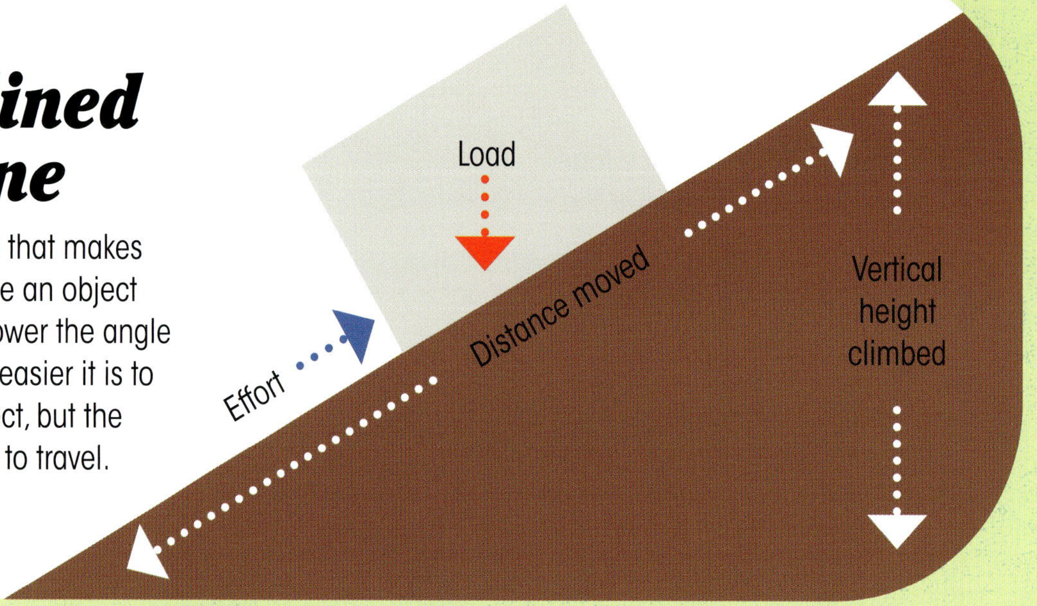

10: *Wedge*

An object with one thin edge and one thick edge. A wedge works by diverting the direction of a force. For example, an axe diverts the downward force of a blow sideways to split apart wood.

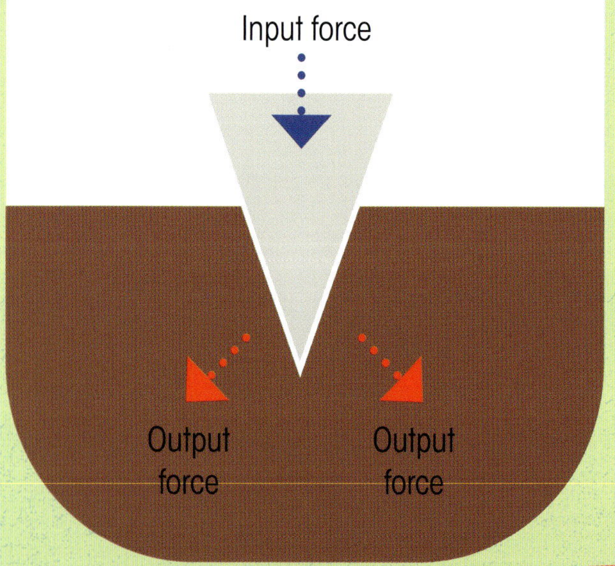

11: *Screw*

A type of inclined plane that is wrapped in a spiral around a central core. It converts a turning force into a push or pull force.

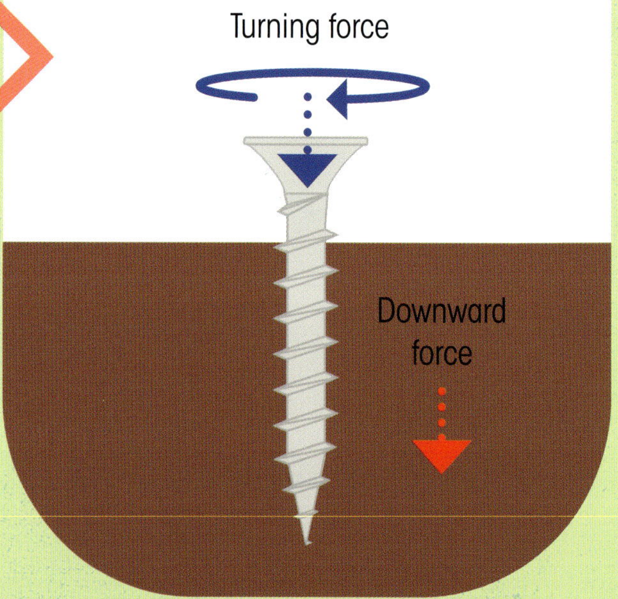

12: Lever

A bar or platform that moves around a fulcrum to move a load. By changing the distances between the load and fulcrum and the effort and fulcrum, you can magnify the effort force, or increase the distance moved.

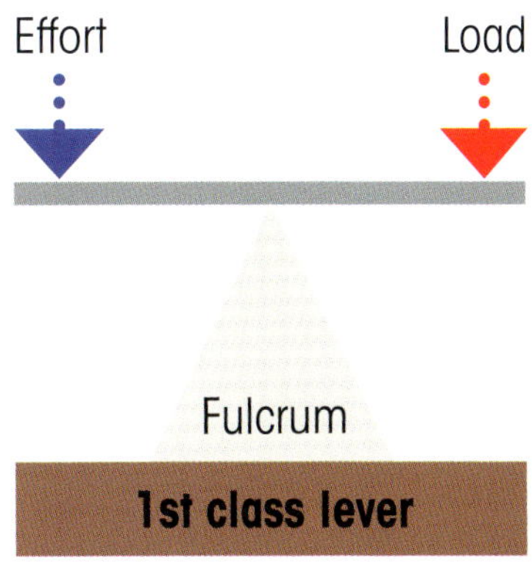

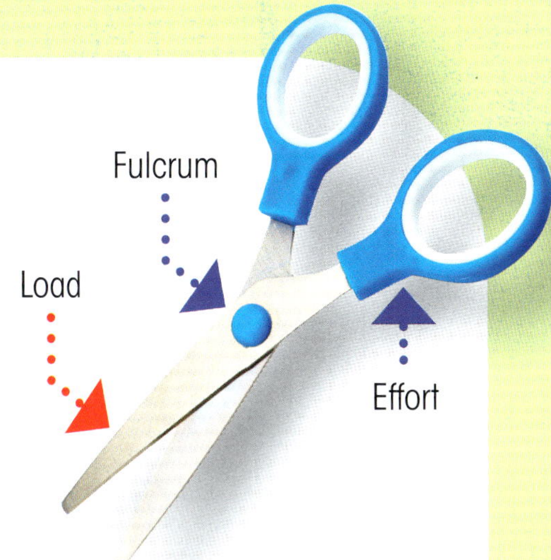

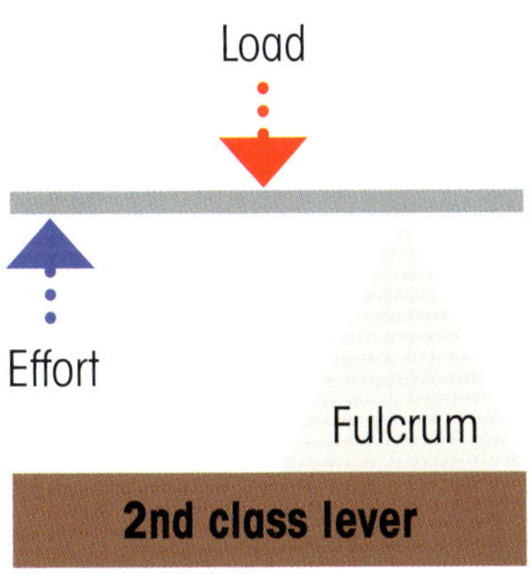

13: Fulcrum

Also known as a pivot, this is the point around which a lever moves.

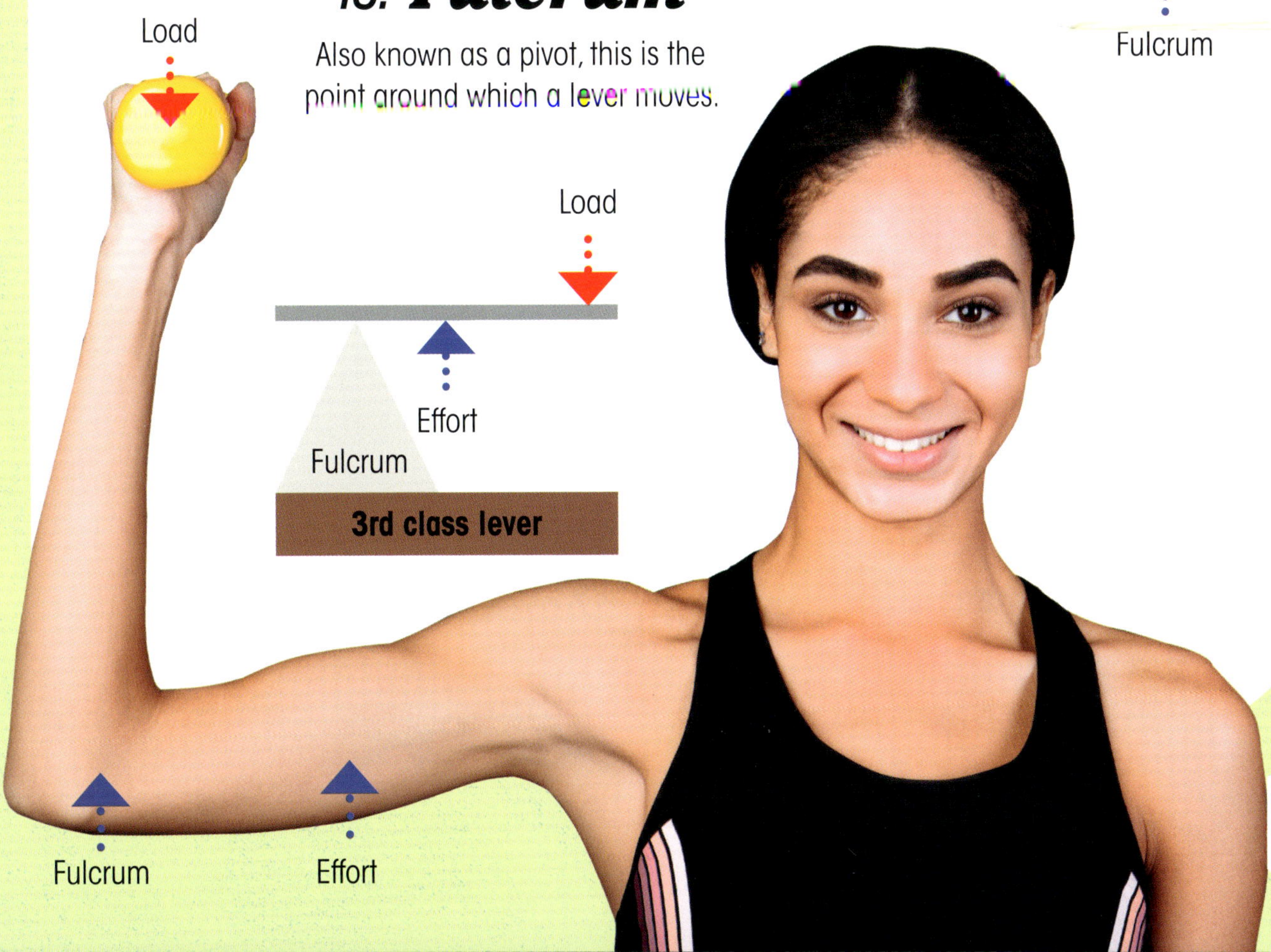

HYDRAULICS AND PNEUMATICS

Water and air can be used to transmit forces, and to change the size of an effort force.

14: *Hydraulic*

A device that uses liquids to transmit force. A simple hydraulic system consists of two cylinders and pistons, joined by pipes containing a liquid. The force applied to one piston is transmitted to the other. If the second piston is larger than the first, the force is magnified but it does not move as far. The word "hydraulic" comes from the Greek *hudraulikos*, meaning "water (*hudro*) pipe (*aulos*)."

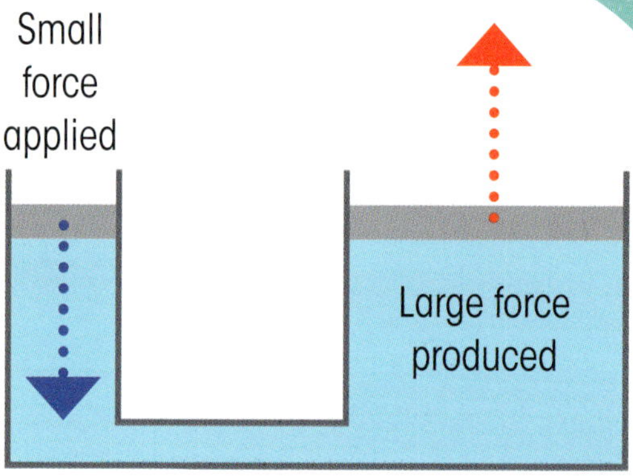

FANTASTIC FACT

The powerful Bucyrus RH400 hydraulic digger can lift more than 99.2 tons (90 mt) of earth and rock in its huge shovel. Its hydraulic pumps push around nearly 3,435 gallons (13,000 l) of fluid – enough to fill 80 bathtubs.

16: Cylinder

The tube that holds a piston as it moves up and down.

15: Piston

A disc or rod that moves up and down inside a tube (called the cylinder) to transmit a force.

17: Pneumatic

A device that uses squashed (compressed) gas to transmit a force. The word "pneumatic" comes from the Greek *pneumatikos*, meaning "relating to wind or air."

GEARS

Whether it's for moving the hands on a clock or spinning the wheels of a bicycle, gears are used to transmit force. By using different-sized gear wheels, they can be used to increase the force being transmitted or make a wheel spin faster.

18: Gear

A wheel with teeth around its edge. These teeth can mesh or interlock with teeth or grooves in another wheel. As the first wheel turns, they cause the other wheel to move, transmitting a force.

19: Gear ratio

The relationship between the wheel sizes or numbers of teeth for the different gears in a gear mechanism and the size of the force they transmit. The gear ratio determines how quickly the different gears will spin.

20: Chain

A continuous series of links used to join two gear wheels that are not in direct contact with each other. Most bicycles use a chain to link the gears attached to the pedals to the gears at the rear wheel.

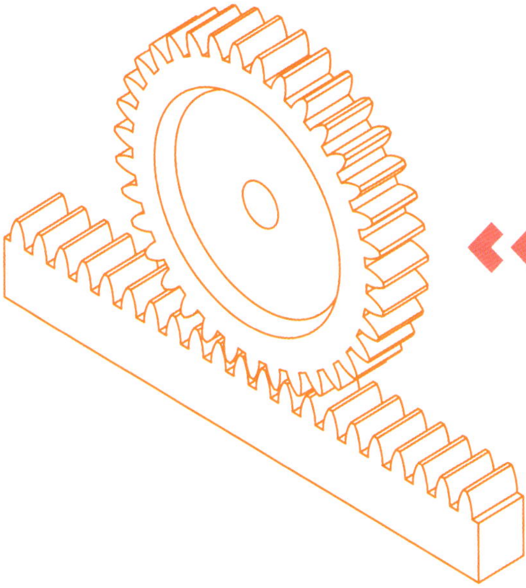

21: Rack and pinion

A type of gear mechanism where a toothed wheel moves along or moves a toothed strip. Some railways use rack-and-pinion systems to go up and down very steep slopes.

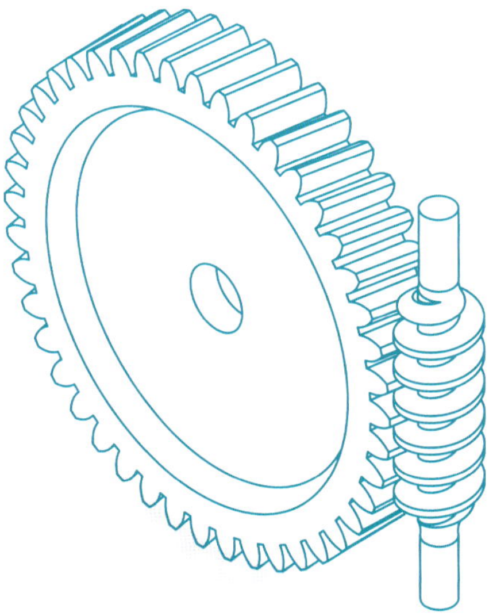

22: Worm gears

A type of gear mechanism where a toothed wheel moves or is moved by a screw.

23: Bevel gears

A type of gear mechanism where the wheels connect using angled edges, transmitting the force at an angle, usually 90 degrees.

BRIDGES

Whether it's spanning a gorge, crossing a river, or carrying traffic over the sea between islands, bridges come in many different shapes and sizes.

24: *Arch*

A type of bridge that has a curved section or sections in the middle. The stone at the center of the arch is called the keystone.

25: *Suspension*

A type of bridge where the deck (the surface) is supported by cables that are strung between tall towers and fixed to the ground at either end of the bridge.

FANTASTIC FACT

The oldest bridge that can be accurately dated and is still in use crosses the River Meles in Turkey. This single arch bridge was built around 850 BCE.

26: Beam

A type of bridge where the deck is supported at either end of the space being crossed by the bridge.

27: Pontoon

A type of bridge where the deck is carried by supports that float on the surface of a lake or river.

28: Cable-stayed

A type of bridge where the deck is supported by cables running directly from tall towers.

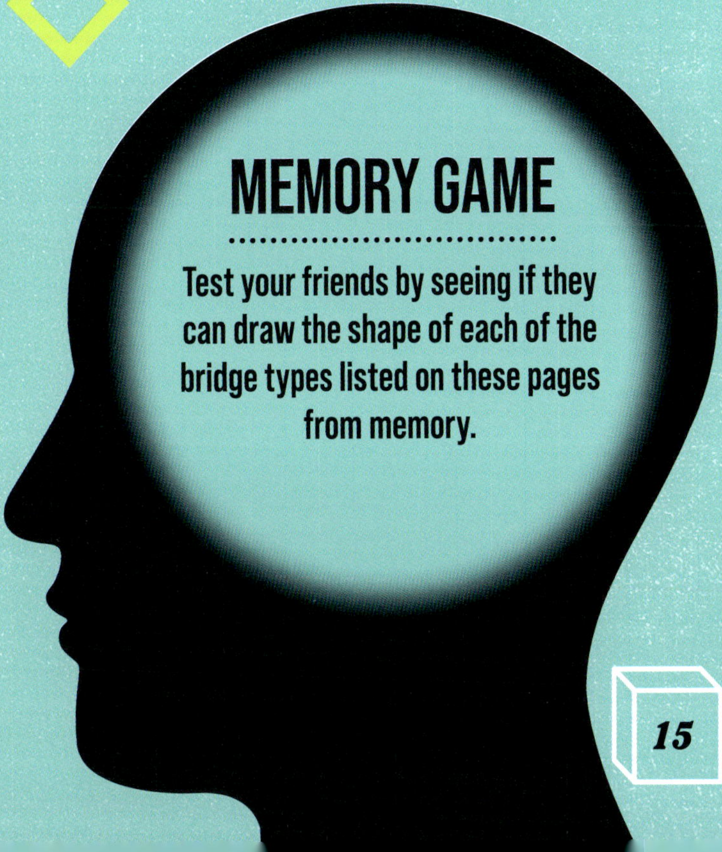

MEMORY GAME

Test your friends by seeing if they can draw the shape of each of the bridge types listed on these pages from memory.

THEME PARKS

Theme parks are a thrill-a-minute experience with rides that are designed to throw you around at extreme speeds and with extreme force. Engineers work hard to create the most exciting rides on the planet.

People on this roller coaster are experiencing forces of about 4g as they accelerate around corners.

29: G-force

A unit used to measure the force of acceleration acting on a body. When you are standing still, the effect of Earth's gravity acting on your body is called 1 g. Accelerating quickly, such as in a roller coaster, will produced higher g-forces. Forces above 5 g can cause people to become dizzy or even pass out as the blood is pushed away from their head and into their legs.

FANTASTIC FACT

U.S. Air Force officer John Stapp survived a force of more than 40 g while strapped to an experimental rocket sled in 1954.

30: *Log flume*

A ride that has a channel of water carrying boats full of people. The ride usually ends with a long, steep plunge into a large pool of water.

FANTASTIC FACT

The world's tallest roller coaster is Kingda Ka at Six Flags Great Adventure in the U.S. It carries thrill-seekers to a height of 456 feet (139 m).

31: *Roller coaster*

A theme park ride where a carriage or group of carriages travels along a small track that is usually made from wood or metal.

BUILDINGS

Towering skyscrapers, huge shopping centers, and even small houses or cottages all use engineering and design expertise. This expertise has been developed since the first buildings were constructed thousands of years ago.

32: *Cantilever*

A beam or girder that sticks out and is only fixed at one end.

33: *Cladding*

The outer covering of a building.

34: *Façade*

The front of a building.

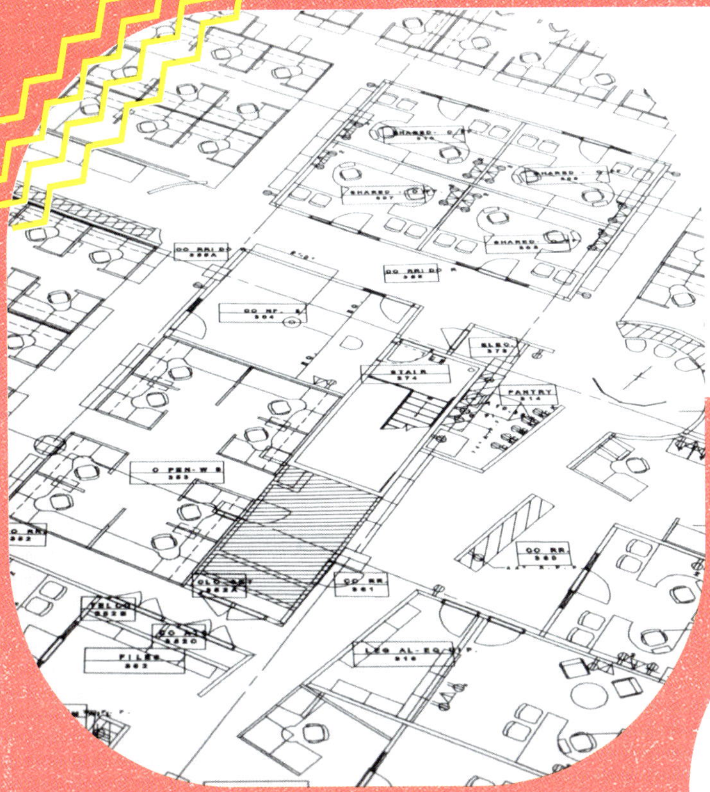

35: Floorplan

An overhead view of a building's layout, showing where the rooms are and their measurements.

36: Truss

Also called the framework, this is the supporting structure of a building and is usually made from posts, struts, and rafters.

37: Sustainable

In relation to building, this is a method of construction that has very little impact on the environment, using nonpolluting methods and materials.

DEMOLITION

What goes up, must come down, and taking down a building requires great skill to make sure no one gets hurt. Sometimes the building materials can be reused at another construction site.

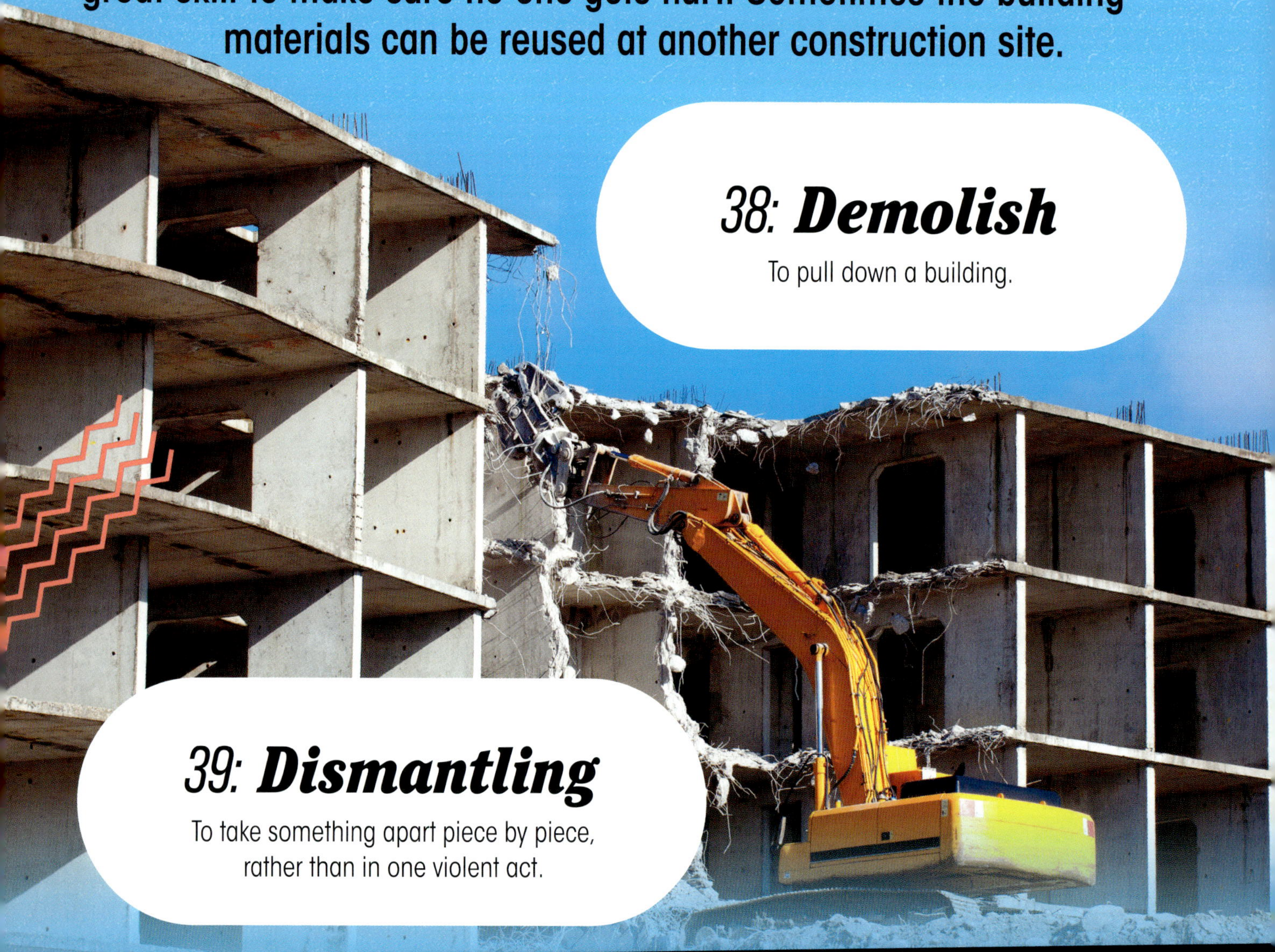

38: *Demolish*

To pull down a building.

39: *Dismantling*

To take something apart piece by piece, rather than in one violent act.

40: *Industrial recovery (recycling)*

To carefully take something apart, so that the pieces aren't damaged and can be used to construct other buildings.

41: *Implosion*

To destroy something so that it collapses inward.

FANTASTIC FACT

In 2014, the 380-foot (116 m) AfE Tower in Frankfurt, Germany, was imploded, making it one of the tallest buildings to be demolished using explosives.

WATER TRANSPORT

Traveling over and under the water's surface can involve small boats and yachts or enormous cargo ships, aircraft carriers, ocean liners, and submarines.

42: *Hull*

The main body of a boat or ship. The hull includes the bottom, sides, and deck.

43: *Hydrofoil*

A type of boat that is fitted with foils (like small sections of wings) underneath, which lift the boat out of the water as it moves forward. Lifting the boat out of the water reduces drag (a type of friction), allowing it to travel faster and more efficiently.

44: Catamaran

A type of boat that has two hulls. Having two hulls reduces the amount of drag between the boat and the water.

45: Sail

A piece of material that is designed to catch the wind and push a boat along. Sails are held in place by tall masts.

46: Submersible

A small underwater craft that is designed to carry a small number of people or none at all.

FANTASTIC FACT

Russia's Typhoon class submarine is the biggest in the world. It is 574 feet (175 m) long and has a crew of 160 sailors.

47: Submarine

A large underwater vessel that is usually part of a country's navy.

PORTS AND HARBORS

No matter how advanced or big a ship it is, it has to come into a harbor at some point, whether this is a small coastal bay or a huge, busy cargo port.

48: *Breakwater*

A long barrier that is built out into the sea to protect a harbor from rough waves.

49: *Harbor*

A place on the coast that is sheltered from rough weather and where ships and boats can moor (tie up and stay).

50: Dry dock

A type of dock that can have all the water removed after a ship has floated into it. Once all the water has been removed, workers can reach the parts of a ship that are normally underwater to carry out any repairs.

51: Freight crane

A large crane that is used on a dock to lift cargo containers.

52: Container

Also known as a shipping or cargo container, these are large metal boxes that are standard size and hold goods. They can be easily unloaded from cargo ships straight onto waiting trucks.

BUILDING ROADS

With millions of miles (km) of tarmac linking our cities, towns, and villages, roads carry huge numbers of people and cargo every single day.

53: *Foundations*

The underlying structure of any building, including a road.

54: *Camber*

The arched shape of a road when looked at in cross-section. The camber makes sure that water drains off the sides of the road.

55: Drainage

Parts of a road or building that are designed to take water away.

FANTASTIC FACT

The Pan-American Highway is a network of roads stretching nearly 29,825 miles (48,000 km) along the length of North, Central, and South America. There is a small 50-mile (80 km) break called the Darién Gap between Panama and Colombia.

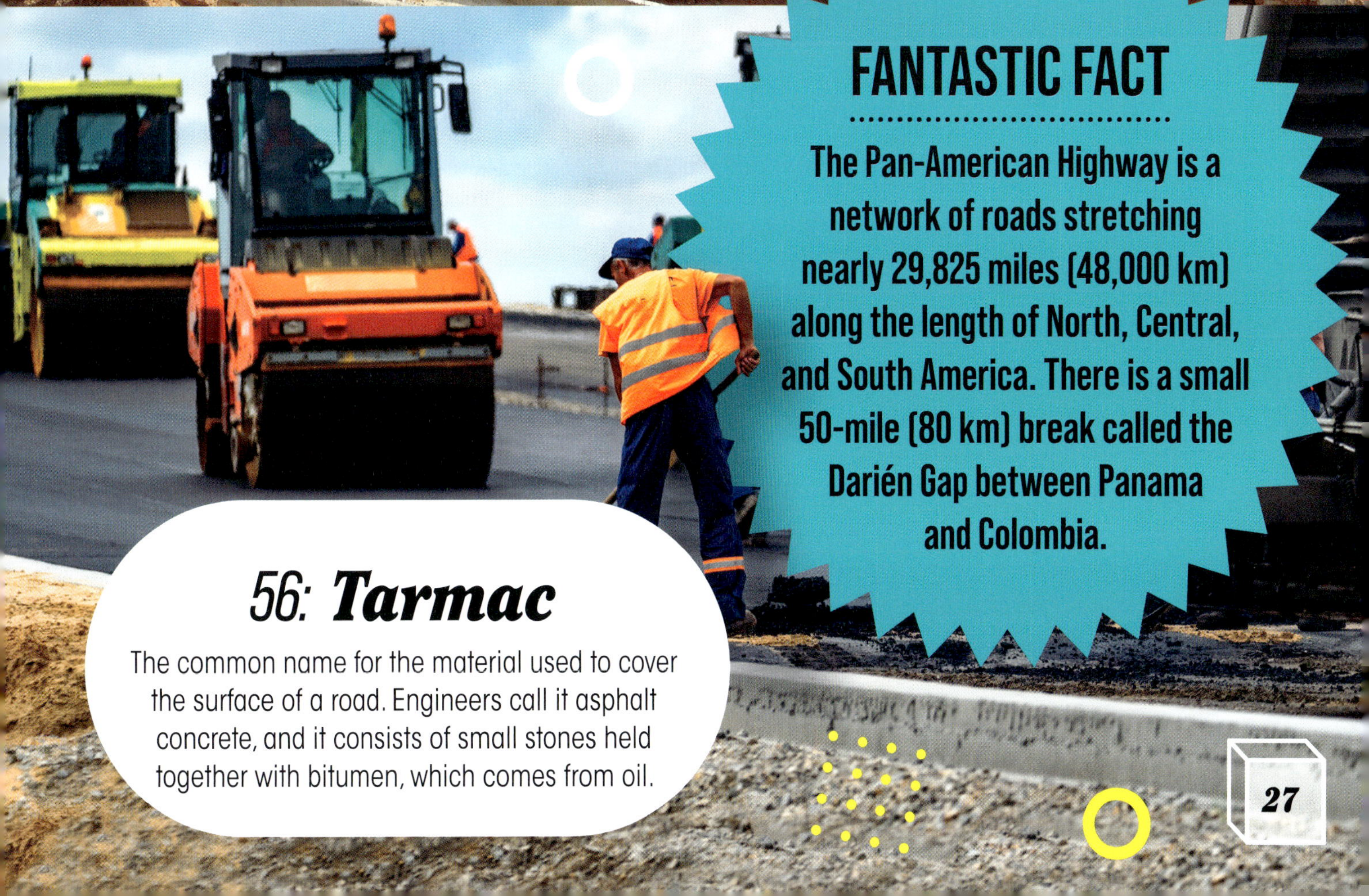

56: Tarmac

The common name for the material used to cover the surface of a road. Engineers call it asphalt concrete, and it consists of small stones held together with bitumen, which comes from oil.

CONTROLLING TRAFFIC

Busy roads need careful monitoring and control systems to make sure the traffic flows smoothly, and that accidents are kept to a minimum and cleared quickly and safely.

57: *Cat's eye*

A special stud that is set into a road and reflects light from car headlights. Cat's eyes are used to show the center and edges of a road.

FANTASTIC FACT

Cat's eyes were created by British inventor Percy Shaw in 1934. It is said that he got the idea when he saw his car's headlights reflected in the eyes of a cat, which helped him avoid a crash!

58: **Gantry**

A structure that sits over a large road and carries signs to inform drivers of speed limits, accidents, and road hazards.

59: **Traffic lights**

A vertical collection of colored lights (usually red, yellow, and green) that are set at road intersections and tell drivers when they can go or if they should stop.

CARS AND TRUCKS

We rely on cars and trucks to take us to work and school every day, to keep shops and businesses stocked and supplied, and to carry materials to building sites and factories.

60: *Chassis*

The internal frame of a car or truck. It supports the rest of the vehicle, including the body, engine, and passenger compartment.

61: *Suspension*

A system of springs, pistons, and cylinders that absorbs bumps in the road, making the ride smoother for drivers and passengers.

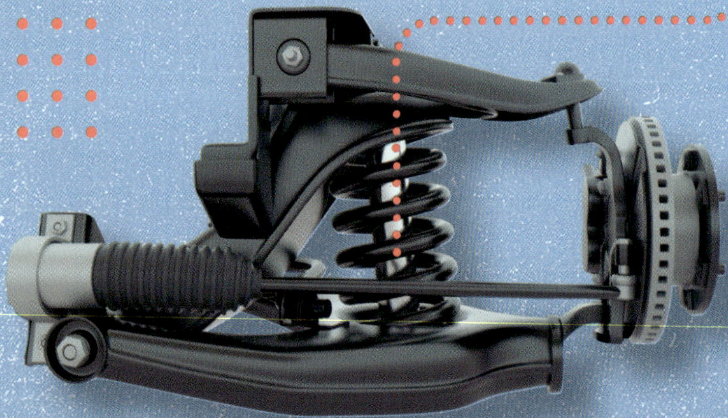

62: Aerodynamics

How air behaves as it moves over the body of a vehicle. A vehicle with poor aerodynamics will have to work harder to move.

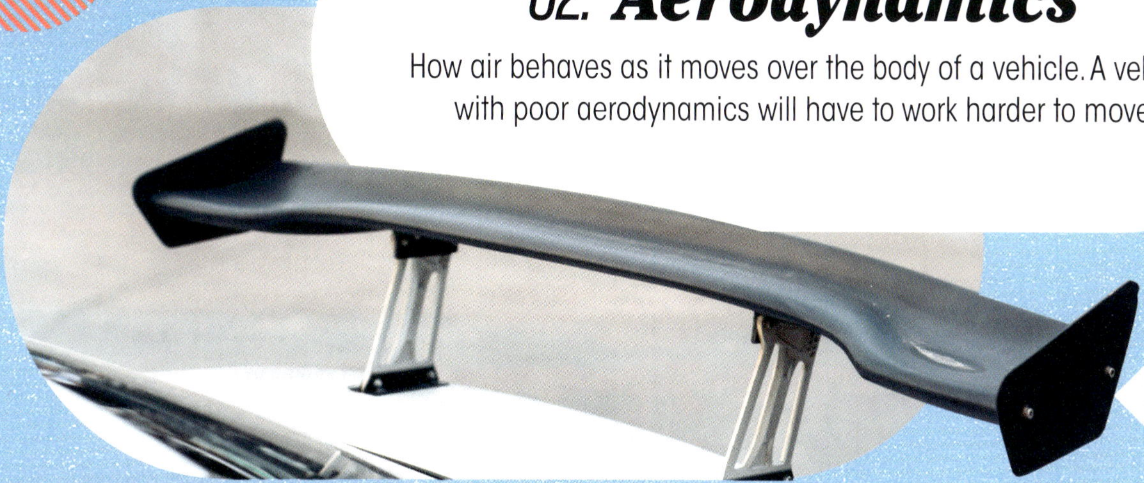

A spoiler controls the movement of air over a car, increasing stability at high speeds.

MEMORY GAME

Copy these definitions onto flash cards and use them to test yourself, your friends, and your classmates.

63: Tire

A ring of rubber fitted around the metal wheel rim. The inside of the tire is filled with air to keep it inflated, while the outside of the tire has a pattern of grooves called the tread. These grooves channel any water on the road surface out of the way, allowing the car to grip the road, even if it's wet.

ENGINES AND MOTORS

Modern vehicles are powered by a wide range of engines and motors, whether they skim across the waves, fly through the air, zoom along roads, or blast to the edge of Earth's atmosphere and beyond.

64: *Internal combustion engine*

A type of engine that produces power by burning a fuel, such as gasoline, inside the engine. In car and truck engines, burning the fuel produces hot gases which expand and push on pistons to produce movement. In jet engines, such as those used in airplanes, the expanding gases rush out of the back of the engine, pushing it forward.

65: *Electric motor*

A motor that passes electricity through a coil of wire that is sitting in a magnetic field. This causes the coil to move. Electric motors range from tiny ones that make a smartphone vibrate, to huge ones that move trains along railways.

66: Rocket

A type of engine that mixes a fuel with an oxidizer and sets them alight to produce a powerful blast of hot gases. These hot gases roar out of the back of the rocket, pushing the rocket forward at the same time.

FANTASTIC FACT

The rocket boosters designed as part of the Space Launch System are the most powerful ever built. They are 177 feet (54 m) long and designed to blast payloads (cargo or astronauts) weighing up to 29.8 tons (27 mt) to the moon.

RAILWAYS

Running along a set of rails, trains don't need steering mechanisms and can travel quickly and smoothly, crossing countries and even continents at hundreds of miles (km) an hour.

67: Rail

A thin metal bar along which a train wheel runs. Rails are usually laid in parallel pairs. Some trains run on a single rail, known as a monorail.

68: Ballast

The name given to the stones used as a bed for a rail track to sit on.

69: Sleeper

A wooden or concrete bar that sits underneath rail tracks, supporting them.

70: **Overhead cables/wires**

Electrical cables that run above a rail track, carrying the electricity that is used to power some trains.

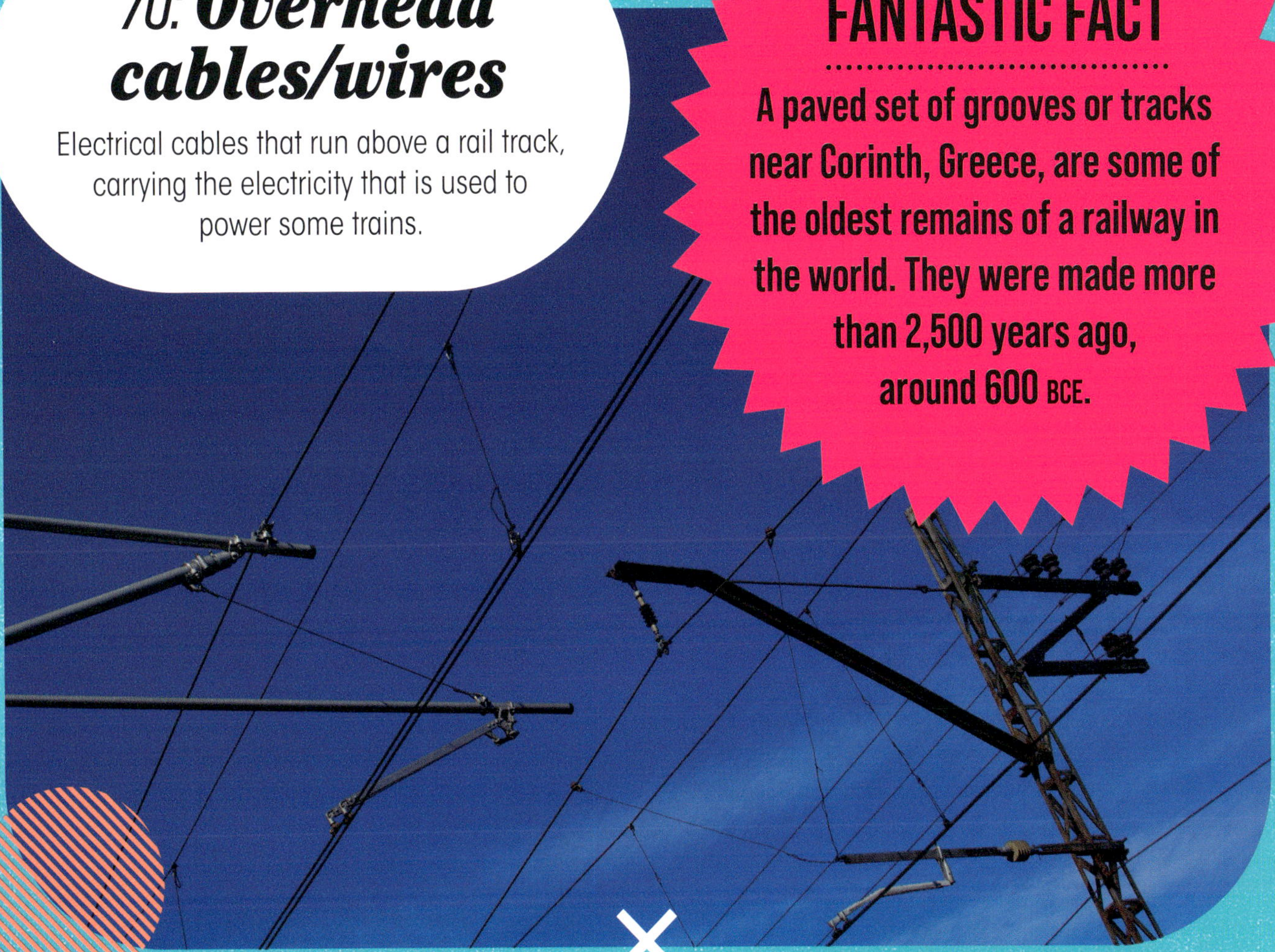

FANTASTIC FACT

A paved set of grooves or tracks near Corinth, Greece, are some of the oldest remains of a railway in the world. They were made more than 2,500 years ago, around 600 BCE.

71: **Pantograph**

A hinged device that sits on top of electric trains and collects electricity from overhead cables to power the train.

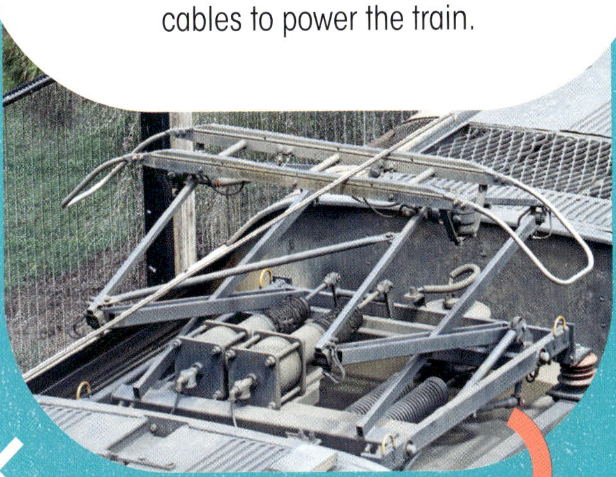

MEMORY GAME

Read this page carefully. Then close the book and see if you can draw your own picture of a train running on a set of tracks. See if you can annotate all the parts mentioned here.

AIRCRAFT

Whether they use hot air, special gases, or wings, modern aircraft are able to soar thousands of feet (meters) above the ground, carrying people and cargo around the globe.

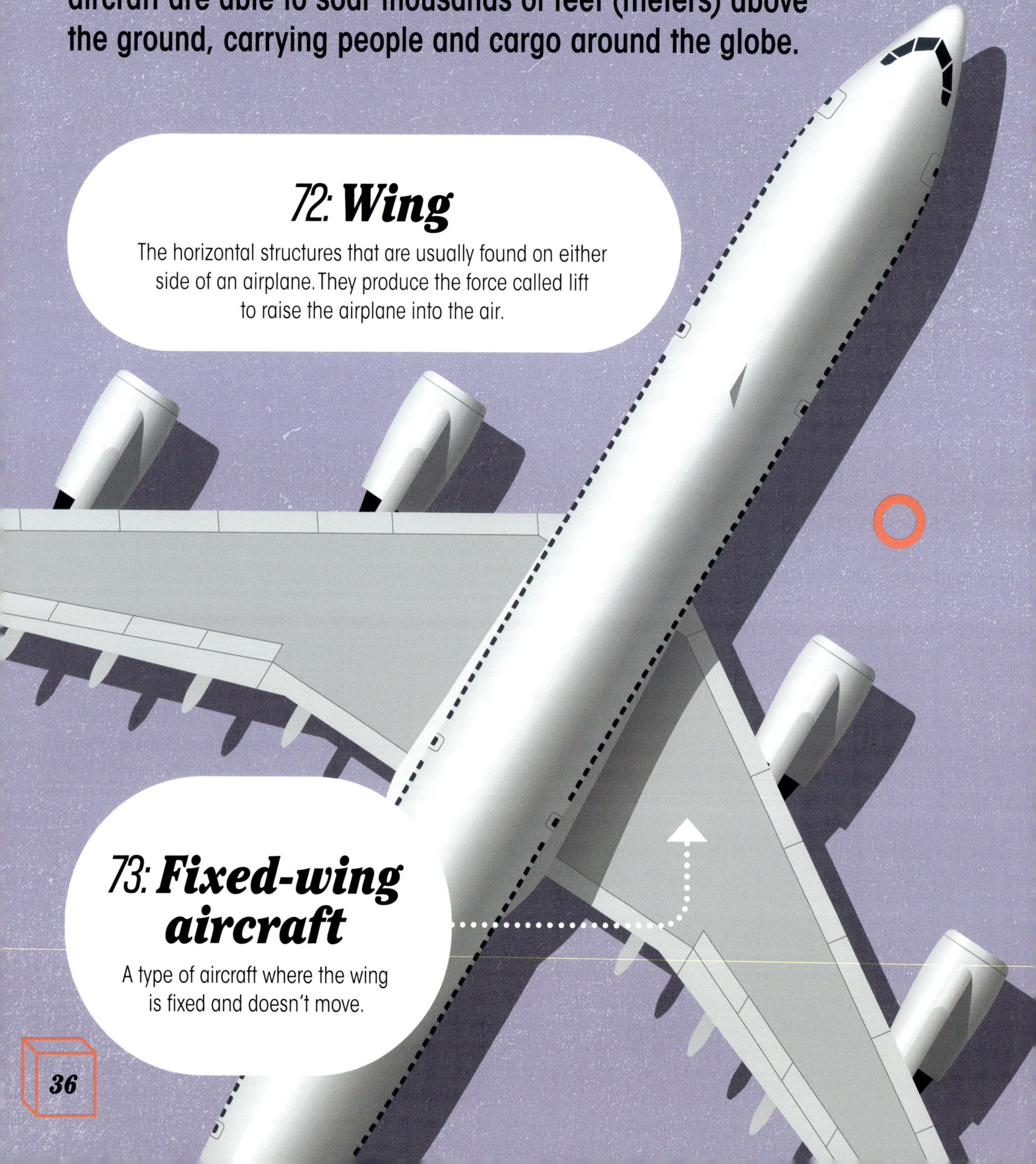

72: Wing

The horizontal structures that are usually found on either side of an airplane. They produce the force called lift to raise the airplane into the air.

73: Fixed-wing aircraft

A type of aircraft where the wing is fixed and doesn't move.

74: Airship

A type of aircraft that floats in the sky using a large envelope full of a gas that is lighter than air, such as hydrogen or helium. Airships have engines to propel them along.

75: Balloon

A large envelope that is inflated with air or another gas. Hot-air balloons are filled with air that is heated by burners beneath them. This hot air is less dense than the air outside the balloon, causing it to rise. Hot-air balloons are unpowered and drift on air currents and winds.

76: Rotary-wing aircraft

A type of aircraft where the wings spin around, producing lift. Rotary-winged aircraft include helicopters and autogiros. Because helicopters produce lift by spinning their "wings," they don't have to move forward to create lift. This means they can hover and even fly backwards.

FANTASTIC FACT

French brothers Joseph-Michel and Jacques-Étienne Montgolfier built the world's first hot-air balloon and flew it in 1783. The first balloon passengers were a sheep, a rooster, and a duck!

ENGINEERING IN SPACE

Beyond the protective layer of Earth's atmosphere, space is a harsh environment in which to live, work, and build. Machines and vehicles that travel into space need to survive extreme forces and temperatures thousands of kilometers above the planet's surface.

77: Reusable spacecraft

A type of spacecraft where all or part of it can be used over and over again. The Space Shuttle (left) was a reusable spacecraft that was in service from 1981 to 2011.

78: Booster rocket

A smaller rocket that is usually attached to the side of a larger rocket and acts at the first stage of a launch, pushing the rocket clear of the launchpad and into the air. They are then released and return to Earth.

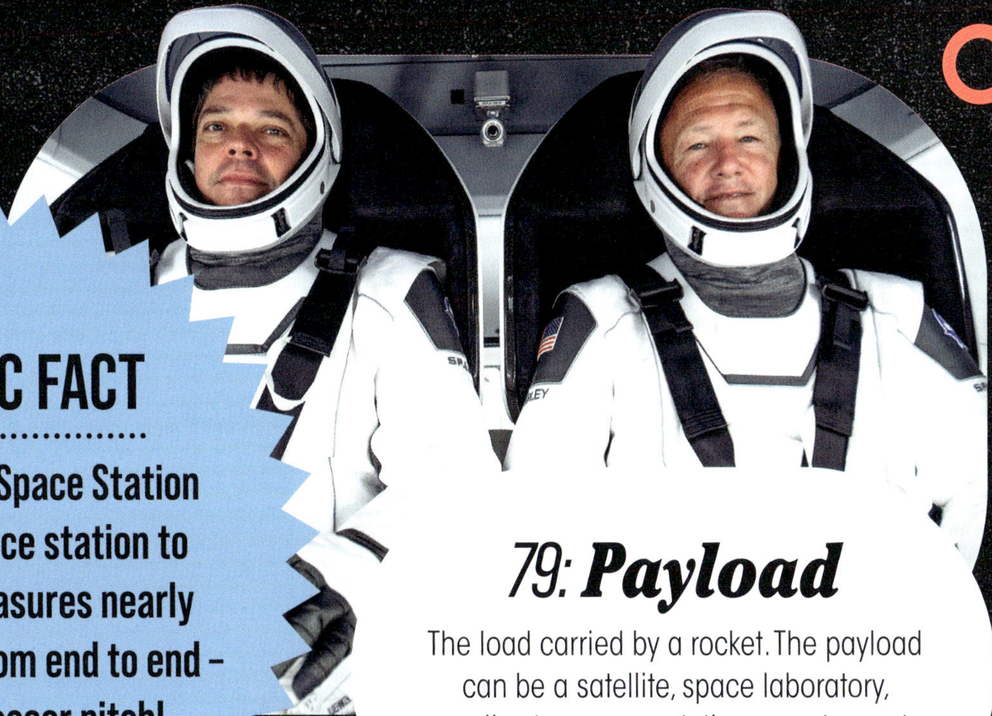

FANTASTIC FACT

The International Space Station is the largest space station to orbit Earth. It measures nearly 358 feet (109 m) from end to end – longer than a soccer pitch!

79: *Payload*

The load carried by a rocket. The payload can be a satellite, space laboratory, supplies to a space station, or astronauts.

80: *Space station*

An artificial satellite (a human-made object that orbits a planet) that has a crew and is used for observations and experiments.

PRODUCING ELECTRICITY

Homes, towns, and cities need huge amounts of energy to provide heating and lighting for the people who live and work in them. Factories need electricity to run their machinery. However, generating some forms of electricity can release huge amounts of greenhouse gases or produce toxic waste that can remain harmful for thousands of years.

81: *Fossil fuels*

A type of fuel made from the remains of long-dead plants and animals. Fossil fuels include coal, oil, and natural gas. In a fossil-fueled power station, the burning fuel is used to heat water to make steam.

82: Nuclear fission

The splitting of atomic nuclei (very small particles), which release huge amounts of energy. This energy can be used to produce electricity.

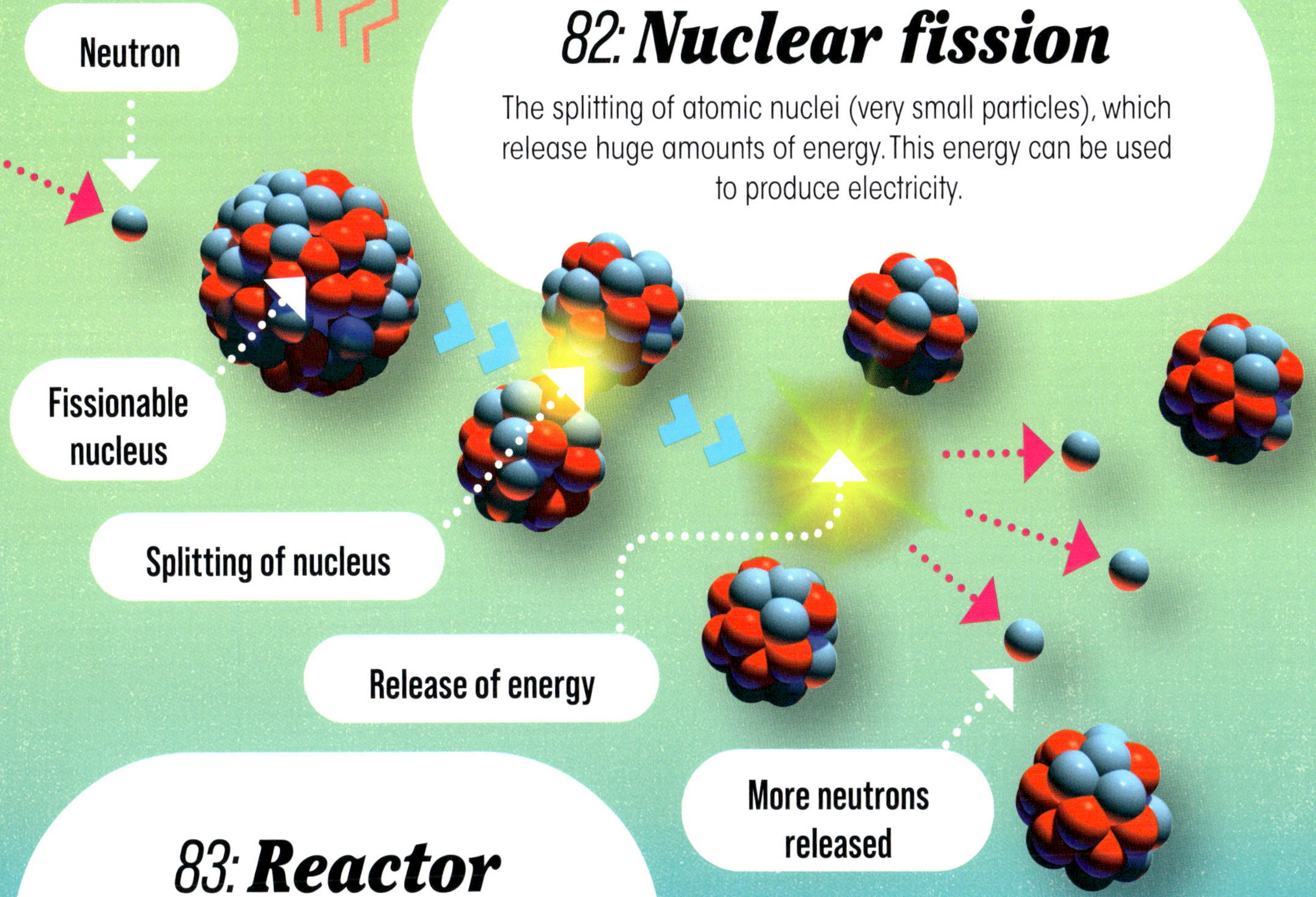

83: Reactor

The structure in a nuclear power station where controlled nuclear fission (splitting of atomic nuclei) takes place.

84: Generator

A machine that produces electricity. It contains a large wire coil that spins in a magnetic field and this movement produces an electric current.

RENEWABLE ENERGY

We must reduce the amount of pollution that we release into the atmosphere, so it is important that we increase our use of clean, renewable energy sources. These produce lower levels of harmful emissions and waste than fossil fuels and nuclear power.

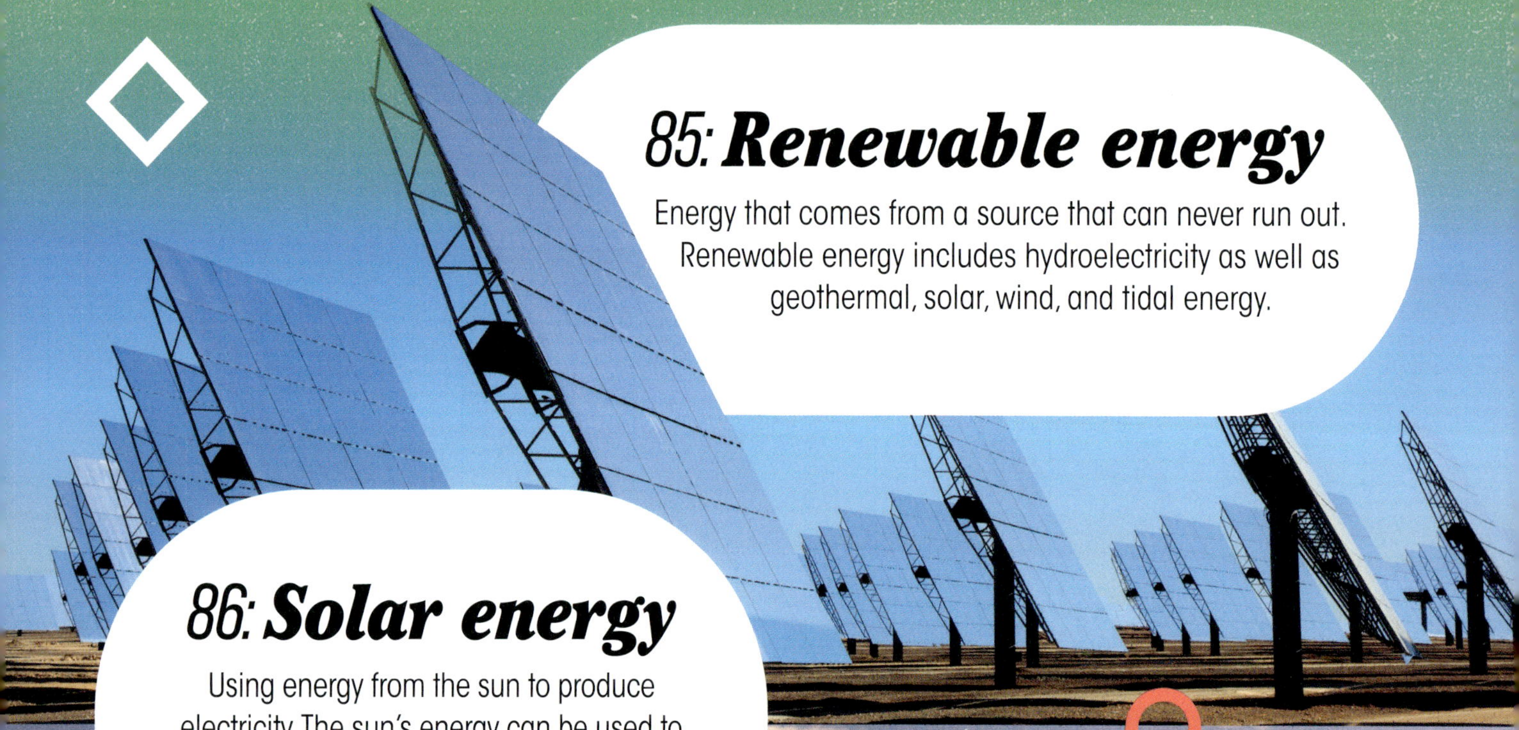

85: *Renewable energy*

Energy that comes from a source that can never run out. Renewable energy includes hydroelectricity as well as geothermal, solar, wind, and tidal energy.

86: *Solar energy*

Using energy from the sun to produce electricity. The sun's energy can be used to heat water or oil in a solar furnace to drive generators, or it can shine on special photovoltaic cells, which produce electricity when sunlight hits them.

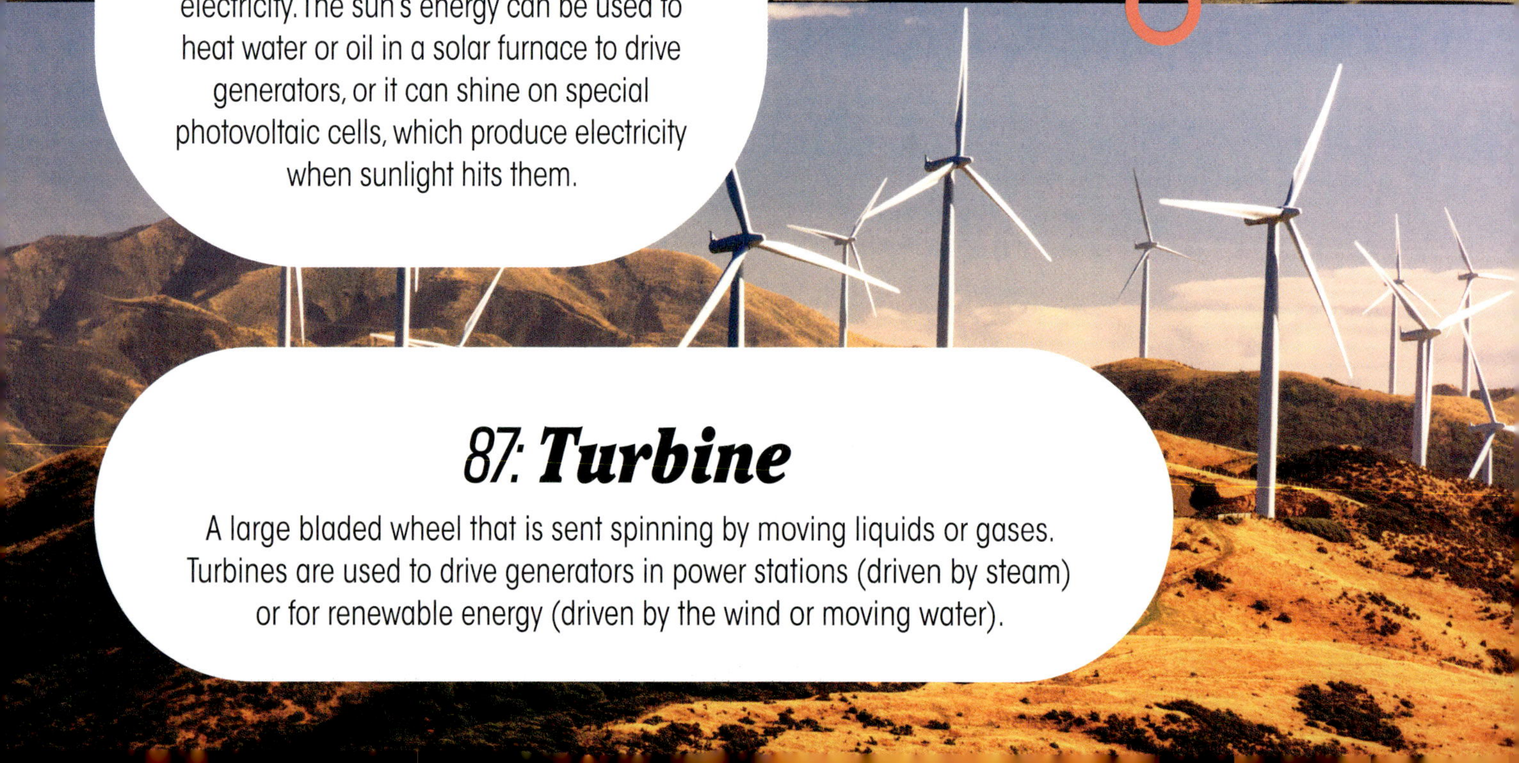

87: *Turbine*

A large bladed wheel that is sent spinning by moving liquids or gases. Turbines are used to drive generators in power stations (driven by steam) or for renewable energy (driven by the wind or moving water).

88: Geothermal energy

Power that is produced using heat from deep beneath Earth's surface. This heat turns water into steam to set turbines spinning. The movement of the turbines drives generators.

89: Hydroelectricity

Electricity that is powered by moving water. This moving water spins turbines which drive generators.

90: Tidal power

Power that is produced by using the movement of the sea's daily tides to spin turbines which drive generators.

MINING AND TUNNELLING

Digging and removing minerals and resources from the ground requires some of the biggest machinery ever built, including enormous excavators, towering drilling rigs, and long boring machines that tunnel deep underground.

*91: **Mine***

A site where minerals are taken out of the ground. An underground mine is a network of vertical tunnels that stretch for hundreds of feet (meters) beneath Earth's surface and even out beneath the seabed.

*92: **Opencast mine***

This is a type of mine where minerals are taken from a huge pit on Earth's surface.

FANTASTIC FACT

The Bingham Canyon Mine in Utah is one of the biggest opencast mines on Earth. The huge pit measures about 2.5 miles (4 km) across and is more than three-quarters of a mile (1.2 km) deep.

93: *Fracturing*

Also known as fracking, this involves injecting water and other chemicals into rocks underground to break them up and release any oil or gas the rocks might hold.

94: *TBM*

A tunnel boring machine is a long, snakelike machine that cuts a tunnel through rock.

95: *Oil rig*

The structure that holds the machinery needed to drill an oil well. Oil rigs can be based on land or out at sea.

CHEMICAL ENGINEERING

When minerals and materials have been mined or drilled, they usually need to be processed to turn them into usable substances. This can involve splitting them up into different substances or combining them with other substances.

FANTASTIC FACT

The Jamnagar Refinery in Gujarat, India, is one of the biggest oil refineries on the planet. This huge complex can process about 1,240,000 barrels of crude oil every single day!

96: ***Refinery***

A structure where a substance is refined or processed. For example, at an oil refinery, oil is separated into different substances, including gasoline.

97: ***Synthesis***

To combine two or more substances to produce a new material.

98: **Distillation**

To separate a mixture of liquids by heating it and then collecting the gases that boil off at different temperatures.

99: **Petroleum**

Also called crude oil: a natural liquid that can be refined to produce different fuels, such as gasoline and kerosene.

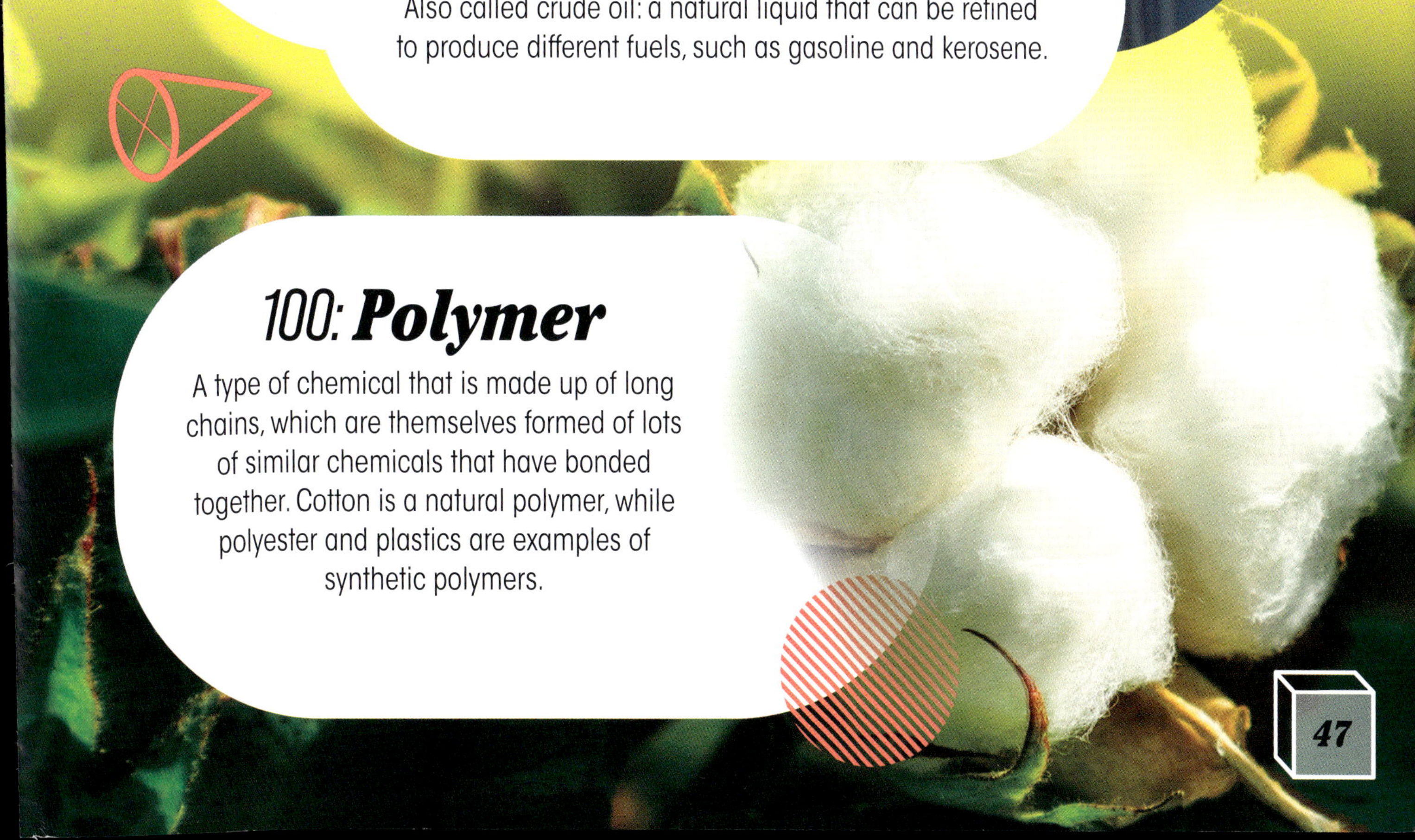

100: **Polymer**

A type of chemical that is made up of long chains, which are themselves formed of lots of similar chemicals that have bonded together. Cotton is a natural polymer, while polyester and plastics are examples of synthetic polymers.

INDEX